AuthorHouse™
1663 Liberty Drive
Bloomington, IN 47403
www.authorhouse.com
Phone: 1 (800) 839-8640

Published by AuthorHouse 06/10/2016

ISBN: 978-1-5246-1382-2 (sc)
978-1-5246-1383-9 (hc)
978-1-5246-1381-5 (e)

Library of Congress Control Number: 2016909487

Print information available on the last page.

This book is printed on acid-free paper.

authorHOUSE®

ELSIE

Jenne Ila Moersch Kostial
Illustrated by David Presley

This book is dedicated to my beautiful daughters, Payton and Meadow. ELSIE was written in love, as an example that you can do anything you put your mind to. There is never a project or situation too big for our God. Always bring prayer into your day and your life will shine.

Deuteronomy 31:8
The Lord himself goes before you and will be with you; he will never leave you nor forsake you. Do not be afraid; do not be discouraged.

Love, Mom

A special thank you to my husband, Brandon. You never doubt or discourage me, and you believe in me every single day. I am thankful for you in all ways, but mostly because you continued to pursue me even when I made it hard. Also, you're one of the funniest people in my world and I love laughing with you.

I could not have accomplished this without help from my sister, Amanda. You were my go-to girl for wording advice and I trust your judgement. You love the same foods as me and share all my childhood memories. We are meant to be, my sister and me.

I am thankful to God for my life and the people I love that are in it.
Life is magic.

Jenne Ila

Elsie, feeling pretty in her brand new dress and shiny black shoes, twirled and stomped all through the house. She smiled as bright as the morning sun and her wild hair bounced with every step she took. She longed to play outside where she could spin around and around to her heart's delight.

Elsie's mother sensed her excitement and called, "Elsie, you may go outside and walk around the yard, but be **careful**! We're leaving soon for church and you must not get your new shoes and dress dirty."

Elsie went outside in the sun and twirled along the shallow creek beside her house. Suddenly, something shiny caught her eye. "What's that?" Elsie wondered. As she approached the edge of the water, she noticed something bright and gold sparkling in the sun.

Elsie felt so curious that she stepped closer to the sparkling sight. She did not notice her new shoes touching the sticky mud on the creek's edge. As she moved even closer and reached for the object, the muddy water soaked the hem of her new dress. Determined, she tugged on the shiny treasure, and out of the mud slid a beautiful necklace!

Elsie sprang up and admired the necklace as it sparkled in the sun. She ran toward the house excited to show the treasure to her mom. She reached for the door and suddenly she noticed the dirt smeared all over her hand. "Oh no," she whispered. The dirty creek had caked her new shoes with mud, dripped on her satin sleeves and soaked the edges of her dress.

"I've got to clean up!" Elsie thought as she rushed to the bathroom. She tried to wash her shoes, scrub her sleeve and rinse her hem. She just couldn't clean all of it herself. She needed her mom. "I'm in trouble now," she thought.

With tears in her eyes she called out, "MOM! I need your help." Her mother opened the door and gasped. As she held the shiny necklace in her hand, Elsie said, "I'm so sorry, Mom. I didn't mean to get dirty. I saw this in the creek and I ruined my dress when I pulled it out." Her mother shrieked and rushed toward her daughter.

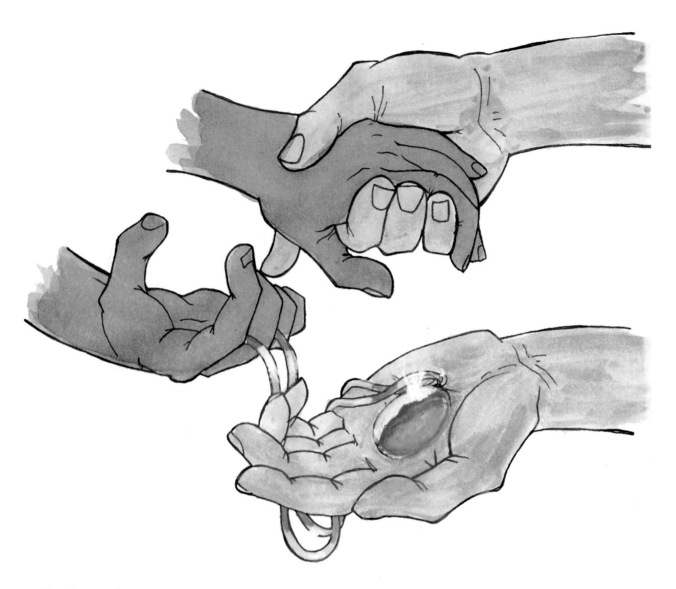

She bent down eye to eye with Elsie and hugged her. "You found it," she said, "You found my necklace from when I was a girl. As a girl I loved twirling in my dresses and stomping around in my shoes. One day I twirled so much that my necklace fell off and I never found it. I'm so glad you found it today!"

"You twirled and stomped just like me?" Elsie sniffled. Her mother replied, "Oh yes, very much. Elsie, I want to thank you for telling me the truth about your dress. I know you didn't mean to get dirty."

"We don't have time to completely clean your dress before we leave, sweetheart. No one will notice the stains when they see your new, beautiful necklace." With bright eyes and a big smile, Elsie asked, "MY necklace? You said it belonged to you." Her mother replied, "I think it belongs to you now."

Elsie's mother knew that stains on the heart would be harder to wash away than any stain on her dress. Elsie was praised for her good choices and her heart was better for it.

About the Illustrator:

David Presley is an Illustrator and a graduate of the Kansas City Art Institute, where he earned his Bachelor's Degree in Animation. He currently lives in St. Louis, Missouri.

Connect with David: davidpresleyartstudio@gmail.com

 Jenne's debut children's book ELSIE catapulted her into a new world of expression and vulnerability. With a career history in pharmaceuticals and healthcare this writing adventure was a welcome and creative retreat. Jenne loves spending time with her family and enjoys genealogy, gardening and cooking in her free time. She enjoys traveling and exploring and is currently planning trips in her glamper. She lives with her husband, daughters and a quirky chihuahua outside of St. Louis, Missouri.

Find her on Instagram: @ila_jko or Email: kostial.jenne@yahoo.com

Printed in the United States
By Bookmasters